Bloom

by JBK

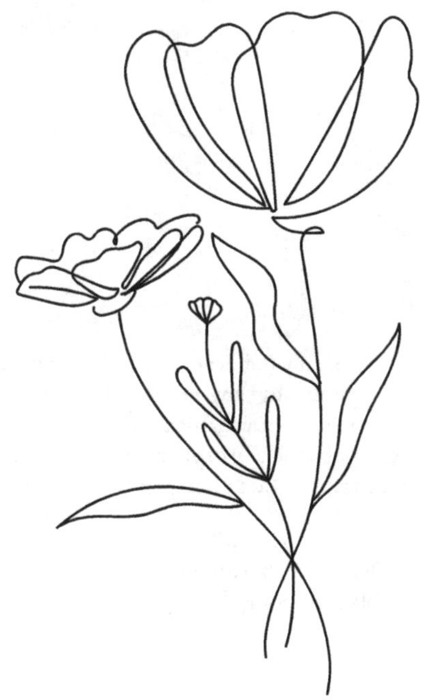

Published by Conscious Dreams Publishing
www.consciousdreamspublishing.com

Edited by Zara Thatcher

Typeset by Nadia Vitushynska

ISBN: 978-1-917584-12-8

"The most important thing is to live a fabulous life. As long as it's fabulous I don't care how long it is"

– Freddie Mercury

CONTENTS

Ocean Eyes

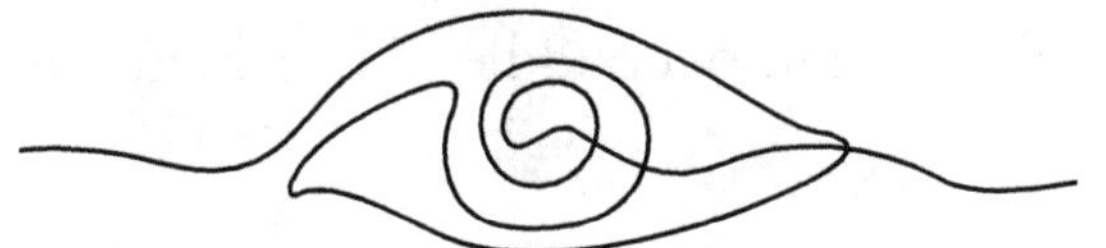

RIP BLOSSOM

Sage's blossom bloomed —
So delicate and authentic
Floweret from its soil,
In beautiful display
Silky petals, slim skin
The wind blew by,
Her hair dying excruciatingly
Sweet became sour,
Refined became contaminated
Her life became a voyage of pain

Her lips were once unique and luscious
Her petals became a horrid image to despise,
Her life bloomed into a puddle of deceased life

REMEMBER ME ORCHID

Oh, dear Cordelia,
Her orchid pigment so dull, so fragile
Her porcelain petals,
Her dehydrated pistil
She looked grave, gone —
But she wasn't grave,
She was well alive
She exhibited the end from the beginning

UN ROSA

Rose,
Their daring sepals,
Their prickly thorns that trail upon their layer,
Death-stared eyes with sting ray leaves —
It was healthy and free
But then, it slowly started to die
Slowly...slowly
Now their stamens dead

BEAUTY BECAME A BEAST

Sleeping beauty; the flower
Exquisite, alive, and well
Her fascinating scent
Of something syrupy, fiery

The wind took a blow,
When a horn fly reached its neck

Her once snowy skin became
Gloom and dark
Her slenderise back became crisp and dry

Within the next moon,
The bouquet of flowers started to mourn,
Started to turn more grave,
Just like she did

A FRIGID TREE WITH NO LIFE

A frigid tree with no life,
Stood for days and numerous nights
It waited there for its sun to shine
It wanted to be free, not confined

A frigid tree with no life,
it had nowhere to go,
no pleasing exhibit to show
It was in woe,
After all this time, it still hadn't grown

A frigid with no life
Its cherry blossoms started to grow
It was astonishing — just like snow
Upsetting of the pain it had to undergo

A frigid tree with no life,
It's new, it grew
The sugary-scented petals have brewed
Sage was once lifeless, now a beauty in the sky
She was a frigid tree with no life

HE RE-GREW INTO SOMETHING NEW

He was conceived from the soil
He took baby steps each day
However, every day got tougher
Monstrous insects nibbled his leaves
The constant bullying he experienced —
His roots dying heart-wrenchingly,
He fought the abuse of scorpion flies

He soon reincarnated
Came back to life
Except no abuse
No pain but gain
Gain of a healthier life he always wished for

FLY BIRD, FLY

Flock of crows
Fly through dim clouds
Always in a band
Never broke apart

Except for the lone one,
The deserted one
Has a broken wing — left behind
No one helping it
How unkind

Flock of crows
Fly through dim clouds
Dear crow, what have they done to you?
Flying alone in a deserted view

He was there, he was you,
Flying alone in a deserted view

FOREST

Stood alone in the forest,
Fixed trees in a crowd
Thick-tall branches that cover the atmosphere
Not one sunny spell in sight
It was all dark
Aspen leaves stared upon her
Cramped, alone, petrified

She was idle
She was frozen
She was still
Shivers creep up her skin
The branches continued to grow —
Strangling her gullet
They grew increasingly,
To the point she could not breathe

The forest looked down on her
She did not know what to do
What does she say?
She does not have a clue

WHERE WERE YOU, FIREBALL?

Withered, decayed, melancholic
The sunflower was deceased,
The sunflower was lifeless
It wanted to be re-planted,
But no bouquet wanted to guide it
It cried for help in the blistering snow
It cried as all the days flowed
The sunflower petals became plump and thin
There was no help for a new life to begin

The days ran past,
The wind smothered the sunflower
Its death was to come within an hour

Suddenly, drizzles of water sprayed on it
Sun shone bright and light
The lava globe came to save its life
He saved her;
Saved her when she was about to fall

He brought back her happiness
He was the missing fireball

POISON IVY

Ivy scratched her fluff,
Leaving garnet marks
It wasn't just a bush,
It was a leaf clump of staff

Squeezed salt water in her core,
It burned — but she wanted more

In a split second, Ivy scratched her fleece
This addiction was her deadly sin
The inflammation started to eat
Sunny, where have you been?

IT BURNS

Fire, fire let it burn
Burn her rumen, let it churn!
The irritation feels so good but hurts
The particles in her throat twist and turn
Fire, fire let it burn

OCEAN EYES

River nudges his feet in the sand,
Shells sleeping on his feet
The cold hits his shins
Sea water in his ears as he swims

Sorrowful clouds, sky's so dim
Barely brightness above him
Wind's so active, running a marathon
The atmosphere is sentimental as it should be

River starts to realise his tears are the sea
Salty, vulgar, bland
Nudges his feet in sand
Clouded mind in a lone land

His chest boomed with allium,
Climate's so fine
His time is blank, his days are still
With his Ocean Eyes

Fluorescence

CHERRY BLOSSOM

Cherry blossoms so precious, so divine
Its sugary scent keeps her up at night
Cherry blossoms so immaculate, so immaculate
The beauty makes her ignite
They catch her eyes, what a beautiful sight
They're so sterling,
They're such a delight
They're so precious, they're so divine

COUNTRYSIDE

A field of colourful tulips
The sweet-scented flowers
With pastel-palette skin

She ran through the field,
The cold breeze that follows her
She ran through the field,
Not one tulip caught her eye —
But he did

BABY'S BREATH

Baby's breath so tender, so pure
His striking molecules
In a bouquet form
They are so soft; they make her melt
They give her a feeling she's never felt

So cramped, so charming
The soft touch on the tips of her fingers
Whiff of caramel — his incense is darning
Pirouetting blobs on the ground they linger

Baby's breath bewitches her eye
The euphoric imagery he creates in her mind
The flower is, forever will be, one of a kind

Baby's breath so tender, so pure
His striking molecules
In a bouquet form

MARIGOLD

He was bold, he made her fold
Her dear marigold
He may had been musky
He may had been old
But he was glacé,
Her dear marigold

His smell was the fall breeze,
He attracted the wasps and the bees
Go back to her, please,
Her dear marigold

Marigold, her dear,
Her heart has gone mould
Is he anywhere near,
The dear marigold?

ALNWICK GARDEN

A huddle of wine peonies,
They're all reflections of themselves —
Except for one
It was deceased like, peculiar
Porcelain, mustard skin
The others were candied,
They were the love of the suns

The crippled peony stood out,
It was in depths of the void
It was depressed,
The others were overjoyed
It was made to be alone,
Set up to be a decoy

The rest were filled with cinnamon and soy
They fit right in; beautiful as they were
But the lone one was coy
It had no shining beams of joy,
Until the day,
She picked you to be her boy

BIRCH TREE

They flickered their wings onto the branch
They crossed paths on the birch tree
The sky was dim, the clouds were blanch
But his yellow ladybug skin was all she could see

Ever since she met him, it had been a voyage
Flying through the gust with no care in the world
No hiccups of tamed spoilage
Day-to-day, their love would uncurl

Then that day, an aphid came
He fought it; agonised his leg
He nearly won, but passed instead

She still flies to the Birch Tree,
Where they crossed paths

They will last forever —
That's a guarantee

SPIDER WEB

Incy, wincy, spider
Flies cemented in a cobweb
It hunts their prey at its most vulnerable
The fly dreamt of Arcadia,
But landed in Proveglia instead
She caught him at his lowest —
Now he's stuck in this wreck
She took a bite at his neck with a peck
Incy, wincy, spider has caught him again

HE

He is a mist in the distance,
He is the cloud in her mind
He is a blanket of calming air,
He is the haze in her eyes
He is a pack of fresh air;
He is heaven on Earth
He is mystical and mysterious
He is a sway of air to cherish

DOVES IN LOVE, HAWK CAME BY

Doves in love
Their infatuation is above
His presence made her feel safe,
No question of feeling unloved

But a hawk became his cycle
Their love couldn't be recycled
There it came, taking their love away
Not even the sun could bring light to day

Time passed by; she saw them both in the sky
No tear rolled down her eye
Just a loud squawk of rage,
And piercing thoughts of "Why?"
It had seemed their affection had gone dry

Dove's love glued in a cage?

What a lie

SWAN — HER DARLING

Tighten her with your feathers,
Her dear swan
Your aroma was never really gone
Dancing in the wind, dancing in the storm
Unprecedented love was the new norm
Woosh

The storm is strong
Oh dear, oh dear
Stay as the glaciers fall,
It's only us two —
She will be with you from dusk till dawn
Woosh

Sitting on the snow lawn
Beak to beak,
Kiss her so raw
Swan, her darling
Tighten her with your feathers,
As you are her prime and she is
Your heaven

ROSEY AND POSIES

Rosey swaying alone,
With a pocket of posies
His wishbone is to not be so lonely

But he's not alone —
The posies are there
They heard his tiresome moan
Hugged each other on weeds chair

Rosey, posies, homely
Devotion for each other is stoney

FLUORESCENCE

Peace, prosperity!
Thou give her pounds of clarity,
Thou are her Holy Trinity
Thy's desire to keep her close to the moon,
Thy make her flustered, pearly & swoon
Thy pleasure evermore adores her
Hallelujah!
She has found her Angel
Thou have the warmest presence,
She endures thou; thou endure her essence
Her angel charm,
Her fluorescence

Eruption

RAGE

Thunder, lightning, pouring rain,
Blaze is the sun that never came
Since the rain,
The air around Luna has been dark & insane
Lighting hit her guts like a roaring flame

Streets over flooded, water splashing the curbs
A flood in Luna's system; her intestine turns
The electricity hit her;
The electricity burns

Thunder lightning pouring rain,
Blaze is the sun that never came

PAGE

He'll chug paper down her throat,
Create slits in her oesophagus
Make her unheard,
As she did to him

Scribble her name on each page,
Give her a slap across the face
Put her in his place,
As she did to him

He'll throw her stupidity out the window —
Like a paper aeroplane
He's an origami — she' a papier-mâché
He'll make her a part of his play
As she did to him

Tear that paper into small pieces,
Shred it into the fuel
He'll throw her into the dump,
As she did to him

CAGE

Gorilla pounding its chest
Roaring out with its cords
The fury in its pupils,
The puffed smoke through the flared nostrils
It rattled its cage — needing to get out
But animality wouldn't allow it to

For days and days, it rattled its cage
It wanted freedom today
The imprisonment it lived,
Always stayed confined —
Made the gorilla enraged

It continued to fight for years and years,
But hunters provoked and threatened with spears
The immense fear it overcame
No one had fought for it;
That's lame

ROAR!

Fear became hatred,
All species of the Earth had heard its roar,
Any empathy has dissolved and faded,
Its hearts gone rotten to the core

FLAME

Flames lay on her head
Her heart churning of smoke
Her life roaring of pain

Take the fire out with rain
Take it out with holy water
Her mind has become ire
She hasn't gotten smarter

She can't help but feel lost in the woods
Feeling alone; nowhere to go
The fire getting stronger
Fiery, smoky, gassy

She has no place called home
Her vexation getting older
Sitting in the hall of flames
She has no place to cry on a shoulder

STAGE

Bulls in a sand pit,
Twisting, pulling each other's calves
They were soulmates
They were each other's halves

Their affection made them starve —
Famished of pain
They need to get out and graft
But their dedication left stains

One wants to rip her reticulum out,
Like they did with her heart
She wants to show them her aggressions,
The calves were an end of a start

Here they brawl — on this stage
They kept each other confined in a cage
The torment they've suffered backstage
Desires have turned into pure rage

STRAIN

Nibble's small, he wants to be tall
He's a mouse, a curveball
His furry frigid skin
His small delinquent mind
Stealing what doesn't belong to him,
The truth to him is blind

Nibbles voice may be croaked,
But species fear him
He does not have wings — he's no bumble bee
He roams on the concrete,
Beaks at the ready for attack
But he knows he's better than that;
To read between the cracks

He is small, he feels tall
His physique is small,
But he's more than a curveball
Squeak, squeak
Come at him with your beaks!
Because he's ready for you
And he's worth more than food

CHAIN

SQUAWK!
SQUAWK!
She's a beast
She controls the Earth's orbit,
From north to east

She refuses for her wings to deny the sunset
She was, at some point, in her life distressed
Where her wings had turned pale
Where her pupils felt red

Her atria is bland,
Her external nares relieve the joy
She's the bird of prey,
Not a pigeon decoy

BRAIN

His plates crash together,
Creating destruction
His melting magma,
His volcanic eruption
He explodes everywhere he goes,
His death eyes are made to kill

Not even the Red Sea,
Can compare to him
Or abolish his face from the Earth
He'll make the heavens feel his ash
And make their safe place hell
Creating destruction —
His volcanic eruption

SNAKE

Serpents snake, swarming the lake
Eve's integument is a beauty
Her kingdom is more than a fake
Garden of Eden — her ruby

She takes over your minds,
Puts poison in your eyes
Makes you hypnotised,
Your dark is her new light

"Oh, she's in dearest fright"
Do you think the greatest had lived in fear?
Her strive will make you live for life
Snakebite through the deer's

DICTATE

His stem ignites,
He hates the life,
Of those who think
That they're in the right
Words stick like snails' slime
It's about time,
He makes the fields his dime
Control, forward & rewind
He's living in his prime —
He's aconite

His body can sweep anyone away,
At any time
Lemon and lime,
Sugar and honey
He's not a just rabbit;
He's a vicious bunny

MAKE OR BREAK

The worlds the shark's bait
It's reached its fate
Mrs Earths corrupt in its aura
Wanna save her?
Too late

The climates too warm
She burns her hands in the lava
We were selfish —
Now natures angered
We're in deep depths, we're doomed
Our last days loom

BOOM!
Another earthquake
No more salty seas, dirty lakes
She's in agony — she's in thundery rain

Stay in your lane
You'll be okay
But stop with your ego
Maybe then she'll let go
The world might be saved
Better than being stuck in this heartless cave

Are willing to do whatever it takes?
Before the mantle makes or breaks

Euphoric
Affection

SYCAMORE TREES

The sycamore trees so fresh, so green
The smell so sweet, the smell of green tea
The warmth is a midsummer night's dream
The aroma makes her full of glee
Bright smile, white teeth
The joy overtakes her
The verdant leaves that hang from the trees
So alive, so beat
Sycamore trees is thee
Thy aura has moulded her
The sycamore trees so fresh, so green

PEARL OF AFRICA

Sweet, beat, neat
Kampala is the Kingdom of the East
Heat radiation hits the tribes back
Sweetness of fruits gives them hearts attacks

Warm glaciers hit the skin
Skys so broad, clouds so thin
Musical beats make humankind spin,
Surf boarding the palm trees with their fins

Sunbathing in the Pearl of Africa
Illustrated art is the Pearl of Africa
Beauty is the Pearl of Africa
Welcome to the ultimate Pearl of Africa

FALKLAND LAND

Souls attached, they're a tuxedo
Even when their Atlantic's melting,
It's their Puerto Rico

The climates warm, the air is hot
Will that hurt their feathers?
They think not

Waddling, paddling in Falkland Island
Their coast is their distinguished diamond
Roam across the borders with their kind,
Untouched, Glued, happily combined

They are a family —
They honk of jolly and pride
Leopard seals to the left,
Their colony to the right
Even if they pass, they pass with a fight
Gay, holly, light

CONTENTMENT

She's the raging sun,
Bursting out with rays
She's the goddess of Venus,
Sweetness consumes the world
She's a fresh picked strawberry,
From the blooming fields
She's a hummingbird,
Whistling away with the wind
She's a honey bear full of joy

BLUEBIRD CREATES ART

Chirp chirp!
Isadora flickers her wings through the murk
Beams run behind her as she flies,
Her aura is palm greens
The dirt reeks —
Her flock overtakes the smell
With their radiant rainbows

Making the fluff glow
Singing a hymn in a row
They're as tight as a bow
They have revered ventricles —
They would never stoop so low

Hatch out the eggs!
They use those bird legs
To soar through the Atlantic
To make their blessed beds
Blue birds — chirp chirp!
Bringing beauty to the Earth

CLOWNFISH

He's never felt happier
He smiles in the sea
The wind inflates his lungs
He cackles with the starfish

He dives in the cave,
With his shining scales
His tail dances with the dolphins,
As they eek of joy

Seaweed growing out of his skin
He's a full-blown clownfish
He's not a piece prey —
He mingles with the aquatic
Spin with pride, spin with pride
Swim from the moon,
Blow bubbles to the sunshine

THE MALDIVES

Coconut, mango, palm trees
The ocean sails within the Maldives
Mint leaves infiltrate the nostrils
The burning climate — so colossal

The sand tiptoes into the sandals
The blue table sleeps upon the island,
With its igniting candle
Herons singing, humming around the leaves

Coconut, mango, palm trees,
Pineapples have society's shell
Iced aqua creates brain freezes,
Painted-on tans, so swell

Assalaamu alaikum,
Greet you with the sun,
Sting-ray, turtles, peppery sharks
Dance with the trees, have some fun

DAFFODILS

Daffodils trail up the hill,
Glazed star shines upon them
Balmy heavens of Casa Gazzaro
Yellow heads, green stems

As she jolts up the bump,
Water falls release from her —
She feels facile
Her heart has a lump of glee,
From his windmill

He makes her sun shine,
He completes her daffodil
He make her insides ignite,
She's the windmill

SOUTHEND BEACH

Mystical wishes thrown in the well
Seagulls squawk of ringing bells
Sleeping on the rocks of Southend Beach
His thunderstorms sucked by beaches leech
Seasoned seaweed hard to beat
Climates not too bleak nor too scorching
Salt water to wake him first thing in the morning
His backbone healing by the weather forming
His brant form is fully transforming

He is glad to sail away from London,
His past life, his dead dungeon

FLAMINGO

Flamingo, Domingo
Foxy, elegant
Charming tone, extremely pleasant
Once a flaminget, now she's adolescent
Valentina roams the seas with her neuter present

Her beauty swings the incompetent fish,
Her flaming feathers is their new dish
Swish, swish — she is everything they wished
They are her sardines; she pecks them with bliss

Nor is she fiery,
Nor is she small,
Valentina's just a raging beauty —
A King that wants it all

Peace, prosperity
Decency, yearning
She may be girlish,
But she's still learning
Her butterfly sails,
After all that burning
Flamingo, Domingo
Her art is so sterling

Bloom

DAISY LAND

Daisies are beyond me,
The clouds cover my mind
Filled with ocean water,
Falls out my eyes are crystal salts
Dried upon my fur, dried upon my paws
I don't feel great — I might vomit the rainbow

The sun shines in my eyes,
The light deceives me
I can't help but feel extinct,
Drowning in the river of white sharks

The poison ivy's scratch my skin,
Leaf marks on my neck, arms, and gums
Scrubbing my throat with lavender soap,
It's now filled with foam

Oak trees sway with my heart,
My daisy has splinters
Daisy, daisy, daisy
Why did the rain take your petals?

I sit on the log near my river,
I stare into my reflection that deflects my future
As the fishes hold my vocals

Daisies are beyond me,
The heavens of the clouds are no longer in sight
The height, my night
There are no more days —
Just murk

SHE'S MISSING IN A SWAMP OF GRIM AND DIRT

My heart wrenches,
My past laying in the trenches
I wish I could escape the muddy river
Full of my dark memories, past ages

I wish I could feel the sacred water,
Water of faith and joy
I just don't know how to swim to the other side
Of life, bugs, and daisies

I'm drowning in this swamp,
Seaweed, grim, dirt
The sting rays biting at me,
I just want to be loved

Silence
I drown deeper and deeper
Help me, help me!
Someone grab my arm so I can see the blue sky

She's nowhere to be found
She's missing, so is her heart
She's drowning in a swamp of ache,
When all she wanted was to be loved

LAVENDER

Lavender above my calendar,
How long can I keep up with this bouquet slander?
Seeing the roses in their vases
Seeing jasmines in their vases

I can't help but see the blue moon,
With daffodils touch, I feel such a swoon
In the salt river, I loom
1,2,3 … BOOM
I wish my petals to be deceased soon

Lavender above my calendar,
The sky is orange, the world is grey
Climate change breaking my skin,
Breaking my life, as I skip an age

The waste bin is full of dead flowers,
I was the star of the show
The biggest flower of them all,
Now I'm in woeful woe

Lavender above my calendar,
I have run out of photosynthesis
Now I am no longer alive,
Just like I wished for my petals

ICE QUEEN

Frozen heart, frozen love
Hearts ice cold,
What have you done?
Alone in the Antarctic,
Sitting in an Igloo
Mixed up a potion,
Creating ice stew

You've brought your posse,
You've brought your crew
Hide in the shadows,
Chilled Mountain Dew

My snowflake hands
My cold vessels
You tricked the sun —
You said I was special
Why would you lie?
Melded me into an ice queen
No ice glacier can be melted,
With coals steam
Frozen heart, frozen love
Hearts ice cold,
What have you done?

BUTTERFLY

I'm a hungry little caterpillar,
Waiting to be fed
To be put on the Quercus leaf,
To be put to bed

The days grew older and so did I
My new bedtime renewed to midnight
I started to feel more thick than thin,
I started to feel euphoria —
Hope for a new life to begin

I started developing a shell of insecurities
I hid away from the shine,
Annoyance built upon me
My mind was dirt — not a clean dime

The shell became vastly full
I started to shell away
My cocoon was brick, stiff like a stick
I questioned what life had really meant

The clock ran away,
I was in desperate need
For my armour to crack
To break from the clay
Eventually it did
Right there, the cracks had laid

I became an art piece
I flew to the light
My metamorphosis finally was right
I flew to my new life
My thorax became mine

Fly high butterfly
Fly high to the light

Fly high butterfly
Fly high to the light

I LOVE YOU, SUN

Sunflower, her superpower
Her beauteous brown eyes
With her blonde petals
She's the shooting star,
That relaxes the clouds
Her slim body
Her snatching aura
She has her clouds —
Hides in the weeds to survive
She's sweeter than any beehive
She makes me swing,
She makes me prance
The Sunlight of our romance

I LOVE YOU, MOON

He's the weeds that protects me,
In summer, spring, fall breeze
When the winter comes,
He brings the heat for my pollen
I thought I'd be lost,
I thought I'd be forgotten
But he was the beetle that brought back the sun
He was the one who brought back the fun
Even if my stomata were broken chewing gum
He is the night sky,
Not one star has caught my stamen,
But he did —
The Moonlight of our romance

POISON LOVE

Resting in a pile of leaves,
Crisp like sand
Why won't you offer,
Your vineyard hands?

I know you're poisonous
I know you're cruel,
I know you're hurtful,
But you're my unhealthy jewel

You've burnt me many times,
But I like the way you hurt
The tips of your leaf,
Makes my skin turn

All this aloe vera
Can't get rid of the bumps
Look in ocean's mirror,
Do I really enjoy these stumps?

Sublime, mime, chime
Our cycles on rewind
Sweet like honey,
Sour like lime
I'm the only one,
The dawning dime

SUNRISE

Swim in the clouds,
Back strokes in the orange
Star gazing the shadows
Of the willow trees

The oceans so warm
The Saffron's so cool
Is that what I think it is?
Teardrops of scented lavender

Rainbow blended,
Creating paints spill
In the heavens of the sky
Clouds driving past each other

There the star sits,
In the middle of the canvas
It rises upon the earth,
In glistened display

DOWN BY THE RIVERSIDE

The water's pulling me
Hugging onto my legs
I'm fighting for my life
The rivers filling me stomach
Dirt jabbed into my eyes
I'm trying to swim up
But my tail has splinters

SOMEBODY HELP ME!
PLEASE
I'M SINKING
I'm sinking
I'm...

AUTUMN & FALL

The fall leaves drop from the
Thick-tough tree
It's varied shades;
Hazelnut, emerald, army green
They sleep peachy on the ground,
Hugged by the whooshing wind

The scent that lingers,
Within these months
Fresh fires warm up the cold breeze
Summer animals alternate,
With autumn animals that want to play

The ground is damp,
Rain breaks down upon oaks chimney
Endless stacks of puddles,
That pile like bricks

The essence of mint tea
WOW! It's so divine!
The hints of ginger,
That tangos in my system

'Tis the season of Halloween
'Tis the season of fall
'Tis the season of comfort
Best time of them all

MIDNIGHT SKY

Starry night, holy night
Twinkle stars, shining bright
The midnight ocean sways,
In a swarm of shooting bolts so light
The sponge sphere that swims in the sky
The sun that stares on the opposite side

The lava globe glows in the dark, in the gloom
The heat it radiates towards the rigid moon
The icy evaporation kisses the warm air,
True infatuation answered with prayers:

"Lord, Lord, please find my glow,
Find there's something out there — I know
Amen, amen, remain me blessed
For today, tomorrow and the rest"

Starry night, holy night
All is smooth, all is bright
The celestial body padding my corona
You're a developed mortal,
I'm a developed Bellona

I LOVE THEE

Thou bringeth dragon flies,
To the damp sky,
Thou bring life to the weeds
That seek healing
Thou seeketh help for the parrots,
And lizards
Thou bring devotion to the tropical seas
Thou delicately placed thine heart
Into its cave
Thou make me swoon towards your moon skin
Thou forced your kin to see more than Mine own
wolfsbane
Thou make thy bouquet seem more sane
Thou are the dearest star of my living
Thou are more than space & Earth combin'd

BLOOM

My mind is fog,
My life cycle has hit me
I'm a chained-up XL bulldog
Treated like cemented rock

Pitter-patter
A thunderstorm in my system
Lightning bolts to the core,
made my body shattered
A broken monument,
A deaf leaf

Reached rock bottom,
Reached my doom
My life's in gloom
No space for chirps in the room

Water my stems
Bring back the O_2,
Take me back to the garden,
Make my rose petals bloom

My striking eyes have died,
They've gone mould, silver, dim
The spark is the only thing alive,
I feel my face has gone grim

Holding onto my glucose,
It's the only thing in store
I'm dehydrated —
Water...I need more

I was a mother,
Now the daughter of nature
Being an art piece was my major
My time is in danger

H_2O has become my stranger,
My mouth feels crippled
Losing warmth was my biggest changer
Recycling broken dimples

ABOUT THE AUTHOR

Jhanelle Kalule — also known as JBK — is a young author based in London, England. She is a young woman who creates a world inspired by her life and her own visionary of what she hopes the world could be. She is a creator, an artist, an inspiration, to the people around her who are able to embrace the warmth she brings with her writing.

JBK created 'BLOOM' to stimulate the mind of others to think about their emotions and who they are as people. She has always wanted humanity to realise there are always underlying themes of deeper connections with ourselves and the circle we surround ourselves with.

ACKNOWLEDGEMENTS

I have many people to thank. I appreciate everyone within my inner circle that have supported my work, and who I am as a person over the recent years.

FIRSTLY, I want to thank God and my family, as they have been the absolute best when it has come to my writing and my book. My mum and my sisters, Jess and Joanita, have always been my biggest cheerleaders and listened to me every day talk endlessly about my work and passions.

In addition, I want to say THANK YOU to my favourite teachers as without their help and their support, I would have never been able to survive the horrible days I had to endure over the years. The medical team have always kept me comfortable when my sickness would affect me, and you listened to my story, book and drawing ideas that I have wanted to include in the book — I couldn't thank you guys enough. I thank Ms Ayhan, my mentor, and Ms Whyte, who are true inspirations.

Lastly, I wanted to thank my best of friends. Words cannot describe the amount of love you guys have given me when I needed you the most. The real ones know who they are and know that they've been nothing but amazing while helping me through my tough times.

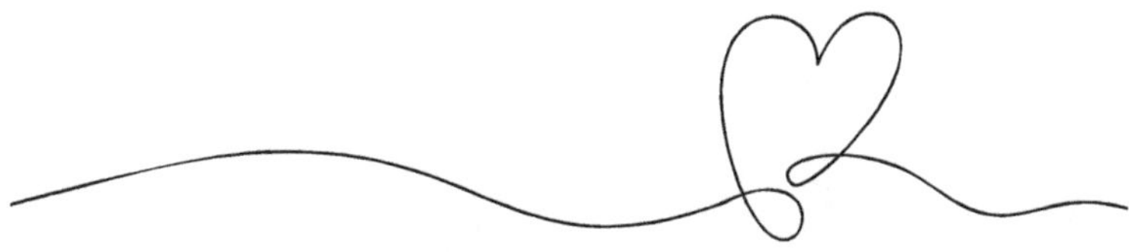

Transforming diverse writers
into successful published authors

www.consciousdreamspublishing.com

authors@consciousdreamspublishing.com

Let's connect